Why Were You Created?

An Introduction to God's Royal Priesthood

Plan, Purpose, and Process

A Royal Priesthood Book Series by:

Jose J Sanchez

Acknowledgments

Although I had been following and serving the Lord for approximately 33 years, a vision of the Lord in 2011 propelled my faith dramatically, and over these last 10 years, two people have been instrumental in supporting my spiritual voyage and growth, my wife Clarissa, and my dear friend and mentor Paul Sherrill.

To my wife Clarissa, thank you for your selfless support. The demands of ministry can often require extensive hours of secluded prayer and study, and you not only never complain, but you also ensure I have everything necessary for accomplishing the mission.

To my dear friend and mentor Paul Sherrill, thank you for your humble leadership, unconditional support, and respect for subordinate ministers. Your influence on my spiritual growth is significant and greatly appreciated. You and Mona have served the Lord and the Body of Christ at great personal cost, never asking for anything in return, and for that we are grateful.

Foreword

The revelation of the Priesthood of Christ has been glossed over by most of church history, but every now and then God will move on the heart of someone who has been drawn to the mercy seat where everything happens. We see this in Psalms 110 when David was permitted to listen in on the conversation between the Father and the Son: "The LORD said unto my Lord, Sit thou at my right hand, until I make thine enemies thy footstool. The LORD shall send the rod of thy strength out of Zion: rule thou in the midst of thine enemies. Thy people shall be willing in the day of thy power, in the beauties of holiness from the womb of the morning: thou hast the dew of thy youth. The LORD hath sworn, and will not repent, Thou art a priest forever after the order of Melchizedek." - Psalms 110:1-4

I believe this is also one of those times. My friend and fellow minister of the Gospel, Jose, and I have known each other for approximately 18 years and have served together as forerunners of Schools of Ministry in the New England and Washington DC region. Jose's breadth of knowledge on the priesthood of Christ combined with his teaching ability are an essential resource for the Body of Christ. I am convinced that the priesthood is an inexhaustible teaching topic that is vitally essential for advancing the kingdom of God on Earth.

All creation is longing for the manifestation of the sons of God or as one would say, the "unveiling" of God in us. Until this "unveiling" occurs, creation will remain in a suspended place of anticipation leaving the believer on the edge of expectation, but never reaching fulfillment. In this book, "Why Were You Created?" is a mosaic woven together to give the reader a prophetic picture and significance of the pattern Son. Jose Sanchez takes us through the Tabernacle of Moses, The Priesthood of Christ, our Melchizedek and the Seven Spirits of God.

Ever since the manifestation of Jesus the Son of God, generations have been preoccupied with the multi-faceted dimensions of the existence of the God of all creation, and has not relented in its quest to know Him and why we were created. As a royal priesthood, we are called to minister to God in the secret place. As Kings, we have the covering of authority and favor of the Father upon us, and by the power of the Holy Spirit we have been commissioned to expand the Kingdom of God on Earth. What we have received in the secret place as priests gives us the ability to open portals in every dimension and dispense the resources of heaven as kings. This is how we are to declare and show forth His excellence and glory to this earth. 1 Peter 2:9 and Revelation 5:9-10 Sonship and Priesthood are eternal and existed before the world was ever created. Sonship started in God and carries the fullness of God. Therefore, anyone that is begotten of God carries the fullness of God.

The foundations of the Priesthood are revealed in two Priesthoods, the Aaronic Order and the Order of Melchizedek. The Order of Melchizedek is greater than the Aaronic Order and the Law. The weakness of the Aaronic priesthood came from the disciplines of the Levitical priests whose priesthood was based on lineage. This priesthood reflected holiness unto the Lord without carrying the nature of the Lord and was based on the law of a carnal commandment. It was a priesthood whose sole focus was ministry to the Lord through blood sacrifices of bulls and goats. In comparison, the Priesthood after the Order of Melchizedek is a supernatural priesthood not chosen by lineage but by intimacy and a heart towards God.

No other truth will increase the measure of one's faith to believe God for the supernatural than the revelation of the heavenly priesthood of Christ our Melchizedek. It is His heavenly supernatural priesthood that enables us to draw near to the throne of grace without fear and doubt, but with a confident assurance that will please the heart of God. God receives no pleasure when we are feeble in our faith and ignorant of this great priestly ministry. The Lord has provided for us, by way of the Holy Spirit, that through prayer and personal relationship, we will be guided into the storehouse of this divine treasure. The LORD has sworn and will not relent: (never change his mind). "You are a Priest after the order of Melchizedek." – Psalms 110 The kingdom of God in power through an eternal priesthood is the eternal divine pattern of the Son.

May this book be a blessing as it enlightens and opens you to the reality of the open door that will take us to another world in Christ Jesus.

Paul Sherrill
Paul Sherrill Global Ministries
Christ Revealed Embassy

Contents

INTRODUCTION

H ave you ever wondered Why Were You Created? Or asked, what is God's Plan and Purpose for my life?

King David asked an intriguing question, *What is man that You are mindful of him, and the son of man that you visit him?* (Psalm 8:4)

Although it may seem like God's intended plan failed when the world civilization spun out of control riddled with chaos, God's Strategic Plan and Purpose are being fulfilled.

In this book, I'll demonstrate how God planned for every event that appeared to derail His plans and how He has strategically positioned people, angels, and other divine beings to ensure the fulfillment of His plan for mankind. A man so splendorous that all of *creation eagerly waits for the revealing of the sons of God.* (Romans 8:19)

With such a divine plan, imagine the complexity of trying to reproduce a living being that resembled Him. What would such a living being look like? How can you possibly develop a man that had the characteristic of God?

Throughout the scriptures, hidden in illustrations such as the Tabernacle of Moses and the priesthood model, the LORD provided a physical copy and shadow of His heavenly plans written in the books of heaven. (Psalm 139:16)

When we observe the priesthood process, the Tabernacle, and its furnishings, we'll discover that God concealed mysteries of the Priesthood Perfection. God's ultimate plan was to make sons in His image and likeness as kings and priests according to the order of Melchizedek.

The reason that the LORD told Moses, *see to it that you make them according to the pattern which was shown you on the mountain*, was so that it would function as a testimony of the LORD's ultimate intention, making sons in the **"fullness of priesthood perfection,"** which in the fullness of the measure of the stature of Christ, our High Priest forever, according to the order of Melchizedek. (Exodus 25:40, Hebrews 8:5, Ephesians 4:13, Psalm 110:4)

Chapter 1

Let Us MAKE Man – (the Strategic Plan)

God is a Strategic Master Planner that has never been caught off guard, and unprepared for any occurrence within the heavens and the earth. The goal of this chapter and subchapters is to demonstrate how intricately detailed is the plan(s) God formulated for the making of man and some of the key stakeholders associated with His plan(s). I know that at times it may seem like God's original plan failed, but you can be assured that it didn't.

Consider this, the scriptures say that Jesus was the *Lamb slain from the foundation of the world*. (Revelation 13:8, 5:9, 5:12, Isaiah 53:7) If Jesus was slain from the foundation of the world, thousands (is not mission/billions) of years before Jesus was actually crucified, that means God planned for the need of redeeming man that would fall.

Therefore, if God knew this would happen and He planned for it or even planned it, the question should be why, what was He wanting to accomplish? The answer resides in the description of what man would be once the process of his making was complete.

*"Where were you when I laid the foundation of the earth? Tell Me, if you have understanding. Who **determined** its measurements? ...who stretched the line upon it?* (Job 38:4-5 emphases added)

God is making it clear that He was the one that "determined" the earth's measurements, an act of planning like a wise builder and architect.

"...let them make Me a sanctuary, that I may dwell among them. <u>According</u> to all that I show you, that is, the <u>pattern</u> of the tabernacle and the <u>pattern</u> of all its furnishings." (Exodus 25:8-9 emphases added)

God showed Moses a tabernacle in heaven and instructed him to build according to the "pattern" God used for His tabernacle in heaven. (Hebrews 8:5)

Through wisdom a house is built, and by understanding it is established. (Proverbs 24:3) *Or do you not know that your body is a temple of the Holy Spirit.* (1 Corinthians 6:19)

God, being the wisest of all, would appropriately plan for any building project to ensure its successful "completion."

For which of you, intending to build a tower, does not sit down first and count the cost, whether he has enough to finish it – lest, after he has laid the foundation, and is not able to finish, all who see it begin to mock him, saying, "This man began to build and was not able to finish"? (Luke 14:28-30)

Being confident of this very thing, that He who has begun a good work in you will **complete it** *until the day of Jesus Christ."* (Philippians 1:6 emphases added)

The scriptures are very clear, God is a Strategic Master Planner. One of the most significant plans that God made is often quoted without taking into full consideration its profound meaning. Jesus was *the Lamb slain from the foundation of the world.* (Revelation 13:8) If Jesus was the Lamb slain from the foundation of the world before the need existed, that means God planed in eternity for something that would be needed within time before its time. Now that is a Strategic Master Planner.

It begs the questions, what was God planning for man, and what was He planning for you and me?

Then God said, "Let **Us make** *man in Our* _image_, *according to Our* _likeness_. . . *so God* _created_ *man in His own image; in the image of God He created him, male and female He created them."* (Genesis 1:26-27 emphases added)

Building off of this scripture, I will begin to address the following key questions:

- What was God's ultimate goal in the making of man?
- Who was God talking to when He said Us?
- What is involved in the process of making man?

In the first chapters of Genesis, we find the account of when God created man, when He stated, "Let Us make man in Our image, according to Our likeness." (Genesis 1:26) Theoretically, it could be said that this is when the process of making man began, however, it could also be argued that the process began when God started formulating His plans for Man. The theory would be that all of creation, including the heavens and the earth were created in support of the goal and objective of making man in God's image and likeness.

As already illustrated, God is clearly a planner; in speaking to Jeremiah, He said "I know the thoughts" (plans) "that I think towards you says the LORD." (Jeremiah 29:11) David wrote "Your eyes saw my substance, being yet unformed. And in Your book they all were written, the days fashioned for me, when as of yet there were none of them." (Psalm 139:16) All "the days fashioned for me, when as of yet there were none of them" means God planned extensively to ensure fulfillment of His plans for you and me. The fact that he said "let them have dominion over…all the earth" validates that the creating of the heavens and earth was in support of His written plans for us. (Genesis 1:26) Imagine that, God created the heavens and the earth for you and me, in order to fulfill His desire (plan) for us, He created the creation, which is why creation responds to us, it was created for us.

In the 8th Psalm, David's questions and statements further support this theory that all of creation was created to support God's plan for creating and making man. *What is man that You are mindful of him, and the son of man that You visit him? …You have made him to have dominion over the works of Your hands; You have put all things under his feet."* (Psalm 8: 4-6)

The fact that God made man have dominion over the works of His hands, and that He is a planner, means that creation was fashioned in support of God's plan for man. This helps to explain why *creation eagerly waits for the revealing of the sons of God."* (Romans 8:19) All of creation was created for this purpose.

For many years I had understood that this process of "making man" had been completed instantaneously in the next verse of Genesis chapter 1, "so God created man in His own image; in the image of God He created him; male and female He created them." (Genesis 1:27)

However, once I understood man was developing Christlike character traits, it became clear that there was a process in the maturing and "making" of man. Man was on a quest to become "Christlike."
From a natural or earthly perspective, the most desirable and holy place anyone could hope to be is in the Holy of Holies within the tabernacle of Moses. In order for an individual to be qualified for entering the Holy of Holies where the manifest presence of God dwells, he (or she) must meet multiple requirements, one of which is maturity. Maturity is accomplished through the process of time and is part of the Let Us "make" man process formulated by God.

A close review of the scriptures will reveal that the acts of "creating" and/or "making referenced in Genesis are completely different and separate acts.

The acts of creating and making can be differentiated as completely separate actions by the fact they are separately referenced in a single statement; "He rested from all His work which God had **created** and **made**." (Genesis 2:4 emphases added) The word "made" can be better understood as something that was "accomplished" over the process of time and formulated from something that had been "created."

Being "created" in His image can be "instantaneous," while being "made" in His likeness," requires the "completion of a process." being in God's "image" relates to His "divine Light" (the knowledge of Him, the revelation of Jesus Christ, the new birth of seeing that Jesus explained to Nicodemus (John 3:1-21)) and being in His "likeness" relates to partaking in His "divine nature," righteous and just "character" traits that have caused us to escape the corruption of darkness. (2 Peter 1:3-9)

There are significant character traits that man can only develop and/or learn through experiences, such as when Jesus, the "Son of **Man**," "learned obedience," and was made "perfect through sufferings." (Hebrews 5:8, 2:10) Jesus, not the "Son of God" in His divinity, but the "Son of Man," in His humanity, in the form and likeness of His brethren, had to "learn" and be "perfected."

The word "perfect" in Hebrews 2:10 literally means "to accomplish" or "to make complete," indicating a result having been completed through a process. This refers to having fully developed, being mature, "a perfect man, to the measure of the stature of the fullness of Christ," which brings clarity to Christ's command, "be perfect." (Ephesians 4:13,

Matthew 5:48)

The word "day" in the first few chapters of Genesis has to be understood as not meaning 24 hours. This can be easily understood by the fact that 24 hours is based upon the rising and setting of the sun. However, the sun and moon were not made until the 4th "day" and therefore a 24-hour time period or clock had not yet existed. When the scriptures state that the "evening" and "morning" were the first, second, or third "day," it is stating a beginning and end of a time. Within this time, something is "unveiled or revealed" (in the morning) out of a mysterious or naturally incomprehensible unseen realm (the evening).

In the "evening," an unknown, mysterious, and yet unseen thing, is going to be formulated and ultimately revealed and visible upon its completion in the "morning." We do not yet accurately know how long this time is, but it helps to explain the scriptures which states, "with the Lord one day is as a thousand years, and a thousand years as one day." (Psalm 90:4, 2 Peter 3:9) For all we know, these "days" could have been thousands, millions, or billions of years. One thing is for sure, it was not a 24-hour time clock which is the foundation of a 365-day year, since that measurement of time wasn't created until the 4th "day." (Genesis 1:14-19)

So, what we can clearly see here is that God has detailed plans, and these plans involve something being accomplished over some time through having completed an orchestrated process.

Tutors and Governors

When God said, "let Us make man," who were the "Us" He was talking to?

First, we must notice that He did NOT say let Us "create" man, but He said let Us "make" man. As we've already begun to recognize, there is a difference between create and make. It has often been taught that only God has creative abilities. However, is there anything impossible to God? If not, then God can create something and grant it creative authority and power.

The implication is that some of God's creations have various levels of authority and power. This is clearly evident by observing the Hosts of heaven commonly referred to as angels. The archangel Michael, respecting the authority and dignitary status of the devil "dared not to bring against him a reviling accusation." (Jude 1:9) This is just one example of recognized authority levels that exist within the kingdom of God and heaven. Therefore, if God wanted to, He could grant one creature creative authority and power, and another creature only the ability to make things out of created elements.

Is it possible, that God was talking to a group of individuals such as a council that consisted of deity Godhead with creative authority and power and others with only authority and power to make things? If so, it brings clarity to why He said let Us "make" (accomplish through a process) man, and then He started the process by "creating" man in an untrained and unmatured stature, like an immature child. Consider this, did Adam and Eve have any experience in dealing with controversy and deception? If they had yet to experience betrayal and anger, did they have the ability to be angry and sin not? (Ephesians 4:26)

Can you imagine the possibility of the excessive use of power by someone that has not learned to be angry and sin not?

You've most likely heard the phrase, power corrupts, and absolute power corrupts absolutely. Although there is truth to this phrase, power's ability to corrupt is dependent on the process in which that power was obtained.

Imagine if God created a creature and granted it authority and power to create things, and that creature got out of control, what kind of havoc could it possibly create? Surely God knew the risk associated with creating a creature with tremendous power. Therefore, wouldn't He establish parameters by which His creation would have to be proven trustworthy of inheriting such delegated power?

The scriptures illustrate that tutors and governors overseeing the training and development of individuals who would inherit significant authoritative positions. These trainees and future authority figures had to be prepared for the positions to which they were destined to hold.

Now I say, That the heir, as long as he is a child, differeth nothing from a servant, though he be lord of all; but is under tutors and governors until the time appointed of the father." (Galatians 4:1-2 KJV)

What Paul is explaining is that although the "heir" is technically "lord of all," "as long as he is a child," (immature) he doesn't differ from the servants and must be submissive to his assigned "tutors and governors." The father requires the child to be obedient and learn from tutors and governors who are tasked to prepare him to be lord.

The "heir" mentioned in this scripture is referred to as being "lord of all" and that this "lord" "heir" is considered as not differing from the servants "as long as he is a child," meaning immature, having not completed the maturing process.

If Jesus Christ is the illustration of being a perfect Son, and we are supposed to be like Him, or be Christlike, how do we obtain that Christlikeness?

And He Himself gave some to be apostles, some prophets, some evangelists, and some pastors and teachers, for the <u>equipping</u> of the saints for the work of the ministry, for the <u>edifying</u> of the body of Christ, <u>till</u> we all come to the unity of the faith and of the knowledge of the Son of God, to a <u>perfect</u> man, to the measure of the <u>stature</u> of the <u>fullness of Christ</u>. (Ephesians 4:11-13 emphases added)

Fivefold ministers were given for "equipping" and "edifying" believers. They were given "TILL" we become "a perfect man," described as being "the measure of the stature of the FULLNESS of Christ." The very fact that this scripture states "till" or "until" indicates that there is a process the believers are going through.

In this scripture, we can see that these fivefold ministers are contributors to the process of bringing (equipping and edifying) believers from a stature of immaturity (imperfection) to maturity (perfection). However, they are not the only ones involved in this process. It can be argued that they (fivefold ministers) have been equipped and edified by supernatural beings to include Holy Spirit, angels (God's heavenly hosts), men in white linen (saints gone ahead (i.e., Moses, Elijah)/cloud of witnesses), the 7 Spirits of God, etc.

At a minimum it cannot be denied that Holy Spirit has been training and guiding fivefold ministers, that indicates that there are natural (physically seen) and supernatural (physically unseen) tutors and governors.

We begin with the death, burial, and resurrection (restoration) in the physical and then the spiritual. (1 Corinthians 15:35-49) Until a believer's supernatural senses of sight, hearing, touch, taste, and smell are fully resurrected (restored/awakened), they have natural tutors and governors equipping and edifying through the natural and supernatural senses. Eventually, these believers discernment (sense of smell) becomes resurrected, and they are equipped to effectively and appropriately interact within the unseen supernatural realms.

Even Jesus, the Son of Man had to go through the man maturing process requiring Him to "learn" and be "perfected."

The first time I realized that Jesus actually learned something it shocked me because I had believed He was the Son of God and therefore knew everything. I had not yet understood that He was also the Son of Man and subjected to all the same things we are subjected to. This is when Jesus started to become personal to me because I now understood how much He could sympathize and empathize with me. Jesus became an actual example of what I, a man, could achieve and become.

I used to think, that's easy for Jesus to do because He's the Son of God. When I realized He lived His life as a man, not a God, I saw what a man could become and achieve. Jesus said, "I have given you an example, that you should do as I have done." (John 13:15)

I had the mindset that he was the Son of God, therefore how could the Son of God learn anything, doesn't He already know everything? Once I understood that He became a Man made in the likeness of His brethren (Hebrews 2:17), living as a man, it became possible for me, a man, to live and achieve what He achieved as a man. All I had to do now, was to learn how He learned, and become "perfected" like He became perfected.

To fulfill the requirement of becoming the redeeming sacrificial lamb, He had to live out the life of a man without sinful blemishes. Only a man could fulfill the requirement of atoning for the sinful character of man. Therefore, God had to become and live as a man with no blemishes (character flaws). A man without blemishes, willing to be punished for man's sinful character flaws, would meet the restitution requirement.

Jesus entered the world as a man without blemishes, but he had to be subjected to sinful temptations and remain without blemishes. To qualify as the restitution sacrifice for man, He had to live as a man and not God.

As a child, Jesus subjected Himself to His parents (Joseph and Mary) and increased in wisdom and stature. (Luke 2:51-52) The fact that He increased in wisdom indicates He had gone through a learning process just like you and me. How did He increase in wisdom? During this same experience in Jerusalem, Jesus is seen with teachers, *both listening to them and asking them questions.* (Luke 2:46) We also know that *as His custom was, He went into the synagogue on the Sabbath day.* (Luke 4:16) These two scriptures illustrate that Jesus customarily went to the synagogue, listened, and asked questions of teachers who taught Him.

After coming out of the wilderness, Jesus read from the book of the prophet Isaiah, *The Spirit of the LORD is upon Me...*, and concluded by claiming this scripture was speaking about Him as the anointed one. (Luke 4:17-21) The anointed one of Isaiah chapter 61 is not only anointed with the Spirit of the LORD, but the 7 Spirits of God referenced in Isaiah chapter 11. (Isaiah 61:1-2, 11:1-3) Therefore Jesus is receiving wisdom, understanding, knowledge, and counsel from natural and supernatural teachers. Although He is ultimately "Lord of all," He is assigned these tutors and governors that would aid Him in living out the life of a man without blemish.

Even saints gone before us, such as Moses and Elijah counseled Jesus when they *appeared in glory and spoke of His decease which He was about to accomplish at Jerusalem.* (Luke 9:30-31) In the book of Matthew, we see that *angels came and ministered* to Jesus, another example of support from tutors and governors. (Matthew 4:11)

The Fivefold Ministry

A careful review of the 4th chapter of Ephesians will reveal that before Christ gave the gifts of fivefold ministers, He first *descended into the lower parts of the earth*, then He *ascended far above all the heavens.* (Ephesians 4:7-10) The relevance is that Christ's descension and ascension activity is an operation in His priestly capacity as our High Priest. Therefore, the ministry functions of apostle, prophet, evangelist, pastor, and teacher come out of Christ's priesthood. The foundation of ministry is established in the priesthood of Christ which is why it is stated that God *has given us the ministry of reconciliation,* a priestly ministry. (2 Corinthians 5:18)

And He Himself gave some to be apostles, some prophets, some evangelists, and some pastors and teachers, for the equipping of the saints for the work of the ministry, for the edifying of the body of Christ, till we all come to the unity of the faith and of the knowledge of the Son of God, to a perfect man, to the measure of the stature of the fullness of Christ. (Ephesians 4:11-13 emphases added)

The primary goal is developing believers until we come to the <u>unity of the faith</u>, and the <u>knowledge of the Son of God</u>, to a <u>perfect man</u>, to the <u>measure of the stature of the fullness of Christ</u>. However, unless both the instructor and the trainee are devoted, submissive, and honoring each other's role, the trainee will struggle in developing to the desired maturity formulated by the LORD.

Historically, ministry leaders have quoted the scripture, *obey those who rule over you, and be submissive, for they watch out for your souls, as those who must give account. Let them do so with joy and not with grief, for that would be unprofitable for you.* (Hebrews 13:17)

Ministers often emphasized the portion that required subordinates to obey and be submissive, however one day, the Lord emphasized to me the segment of "those who must give account." He made it clear to me, that He would hold me accountable for those whom He placed under my care.

Suddenly my perspective changed, the trainee must obey and be submissive which enables the instructor to equip and edify. And the instructor will be held accountable for fulfilling his/her responsibility of equipping and edifying those under their administrative care (tutorship and governance).

The emphases are that we all have been assigned tutors and governors which include apostles, prophets, evangelists, pastors, and teachers. It is important to recognize that these five were given "till" we meet the stated goal. If we, meaning the entire body of Christ, have not met that goal, then ALL FIVE are still needed. If we no longer have apostles and prophets, as some people teach, then we cannot meet the final goal, because all five ministries are required within the life of a believer.

Angelic Guidance

Throughout the scriptures, there are stories of when angels (heavenly hosts serving as messengers) come and explain things to men. In the 8th chapter of Daniel, he sees and/or hears supernatural beings referred to as holy ones, the angel Gabriel, and someone having the "appearance of a man." (Daniel 8:13-20) Daniel hears a voice of a man saying "Gabriel, make this man understand the vision." This angelic being named Gabriel, who also appeared to Zacharias and Mary, begins to make known to Daniel the meaning of the vision. (Daniel 8:17, 19, Luke 1:19, 26-27)

It is important to understand that the angel Gabriel was given the instruction (command) to "make this man understand the vision." No one else had been given this instruction, responsibility, authority, and/or even ability to "make this man understand the vision."

Think about this, Jesus often said "he who has ears to hear, let him hear." (Matthew 11:15) If the Spirit does not give you the ear to hear, you cannot hear. (Revelation 2:29)

The scriptures give an account of God meeting with His council in which multiple spirits make suggestions. However, He only authorized one spirit's suggestion and said, "you shall persuade him." (1 King 22:21) That one spirit was the only one authorized to proceed and "persuade." If Daniel would not have been receptive to the angel Gabriel, he would never have received the understanding of the vision.

The condition of Jehoshaphat's heart impacted his ability to hear the truth; therefore, he was not able to hear the truth spoken by Micaiah but believed the lies spoken through the mouth of his false prophets. (1 King 22) The only person authorized to tell Jehoshaphat the truth was Micaiah, and the only one that persuades his hardened heart was the authorized lying spirit.

The angel Gabriel said to Zacharias, *I am Gabriel, who stands in the presence of God, and was sent to you and bring you these glad tidings. But behold, you will be mute and not able to speak until the day these things take place, because you did not believe my words which will be fulfilled in their own time.* (Luke 1:19-20) The fact that Zacharias did not believe the message commissioned by God, had a negative consequence on him. Fortunately, the consequence wasn't severe, but how often do people not believe God's commissioned messengers? Which include "angels" and men (witnesses, preachers sent by God).

There are numerous biblical stories in which God used angels to guide not only ministry leaders but average men such as Cornelius. (Acts 10:3, 27:23) Therefore no one should feel that God only sends angels to help ministers, but all of His children.

In addition to understanding that God sends supernatural beings such as angels to communicate truths with us, it is also important to understand that we are not prohibited from initiating the conversation. Daniel tells of how he was grieved and troubled by a vision he had seen and did not understand. He explained that he saw "one of those who stood by" and Daniel initiated to effort of approaching and asking him for an interpretation of the vision. (Daniel 7:15-16) Therefore, not only are these angelic beings sent to assist us (minister to us), but we can approach them requesting assistance.

However, we must not forget that angels are *ministering spirits sent forth to minister for those who will inherit salvation.* (Hebrews 1:14) Angels are not to be worshipped and/or become the primary focus of our attention and devotion. They are however to be honored and treated with respect as those sent by God to aid us in fulfilling the will, plan, and purpose of God.

The implication is that besides our natural fivefold ministers, who we are to honor, God also uses supernatural beings such as angels to bring us understanding and guidance.

7 Spirits of the LORD

The 7 Spirits of the LORD played key roles in Jesus' life, and they are intended to play significant roles in our life. The key points I want to highlight are:

- The 7 Spirits of the LORD are not 1 Spirit manifesting in 7 different functions, but 7 distinct Spirits with specific functions.
- They are sent and traveled throughout the earth and are not only restricted to being before the throne of the LORD.
- They are referred to as Spirits, Lampstands, and Eyes throughout the scriptures.
- They are a part of the Council of God and function as Tutors and Governors over the heirs.

There shall come forth a Rod from the stem of Jesse, And a Branch shall grow of his roots. The Spirit of the LORD shall rest upon Him, The Spirit of wisdom and understanding, The Spirit of counsel and might, The Spirit of knowledge and of the fear of the LORD. His delight is in the fear of the LORD. (Isaiah 11:1-3)

PLURALITY VERSE SINGULARITY:

Nowhere in this scripture does it imply that these seven mentioned Spirits are a singular Spirit. The fact that they are mentioned in four distinct sentence structures with an identifier, "The Spirit of," indicates another entity. At best you could attempt to consolidate them into four Spirits behind every citation of the identifier of "Spirit." Example: #1 The Spirit of the LORD, #2 the Spirit of wisdom and understanding,

#3 the Spirit of counsel and might, and #4 the Spirit of knowledge and of the fear of the LORD. However, this doesn't work either because in the next verse (Isaiah 11:3) the Spirit of the fear of the LORD is mentioned singularly indicating this Spirit as separate from the Spirit of knowledge. A deeper study of the Spirit of the fear of the LORD and the word "delight" in verse 3, will reveal that this Spirit enhances discernment and causes us to become quick of understanding.

In John's revelation, he described seeing the throne, and the Lamb was standing in the midst of the elders, *having seven horns and seven eyes, which are the seven Spirits of God.* (Revelation 5:6) The wording for Spirits is not a singular but plural word for multiple Spirits.

He further described, *Seven lamps of fire were burning before the throne, which are the seven Spirits of God.* (Revelation 4:5) And hearing spoken words by *He who holds the seven stars in His right hand, who walks in the midst of the seven golden lampstands.* (Revelation 2:1) If the seven lampstands, which are the seven Spirits, were only one Spirit, it wouldn't make sense to use a plural word for Spirits or lampstands and describe Him as walking in "their" midst instead of "his" midst.

We must understand the plurality of these 7 Spirits, which enables us to interact with them all, and receive what is appropriated to us from them.

God only gave Solomon the Spirit of Wisdom and Understanding; *see, I have given you a <u>wise</u> and <u>understanding</u> heart.* (1 Kings 3:12 emphases added) This is reflected in Paul's prayer for the church in Ephesus, *I keep asking* *that God…may give you the Spirit of wisdom and revelation…that the eyes of your heart may be enlightened.* (Ephesians 1:17-18 NIV) The "eyes" or lamp of your "heart" are illuminated by the light or fire from the lampstand of these two Spirits of Wisdom and Understanding. Solomon was only afforded access to two of these 7 Spirits, but we are afforded access to them all as tutors and governors.

It should also be stated, that since these 7 Spirits are distinct Spirits, their name identifier should be capitalized, for example, the Spirit of the LORD, the Spirit of Wisdom, the Spirit of Understanding, the Spirit of Counsel, the Spirit of Might, the Spirit of Knowledge, and the Spirit of the Fear of the LORD.

THE 7 SPIRITS ARE SENT AND TRAVEL:

John also described these seven Spirits as being *sent out into all the earth,* which indicates they don't only remain before the throne. (Revelation 5:6) This can also be observed in the scripture that says *the eyes of the LORD run to and fro throughout the whole earth, to show Himself strong on behalf of those whose heart is loyal to Him.* (2 Chronicles 16:9)

Make no mistake, Jesus said *I am the door, If anyone enters by Me, he will be saved, and will go in and out and find pasture.* (John 10:9) The fact that Jesus describes us as going in and out and finding the pasture of the Good Shepperd, indicates we can enter in and out of the heavens just like Paul and others did. (2 Corinthians 12:2, Revelation 1:10-18, 4:1-5)

It is more beneficial that we enter the various depths of heaven, experience the supernatural realms, and engage with the Father, Son, Holy Spirit, and others directly. But these supernatural beings also visit and manifest in the natural realm. Do not be discouraged, there is a progression to our maturing process in which those who seek, do find, and mature to greater depths of priestly sonship.

Like the wind that *blows where it wishes…so is everyone who is born of the Spirit*…going wherever they wish. (John 3:5-8) Until we are fully matured, renewed, restored, and born of the water and the Spirit blowing wherever we wish, our Supernatural tutors and governors come to us, lead us to Him, and the supernatural manifestation of who we are in Christ.

SPIRITS, LAMPSTANDS, AND EYES:

The 7 Spirits of the LORD are also referred to as Lampstands and Eyes. This can be better comprehended through the candlestick in the Tabernacle of Moses, the lampstands before God's throne, and how they illuminate or enlightened the Eyes of our Heart/Understanding. The more we understand that they bring enlightenment upon the soil of our heart, the more fertile our hearts will be for producing fruits from the "good seeds" of the "good sower" and not thorns. (Matthew 13:1-26)

We must understand that these 7 Spirits were available and essential in Jesus' growth and life, and they are available and essential in our growth and life.

I am bringing forth My Servant the BRANCH…the stone…upon the stone are seven eyes. (Zechariah 3:8-9) The anointed one, the slain Lamb, spoken of by Isaiah, Zechariah, and John, has 7 Spirits also described as Lampstands and Eyes.

The result of being anointed by these 7 Spirits is described in the 61st chapter of Isaiah, which Jesus read after coming out of the wilderness. *The Spirit of the LORD is upon me, because He has anointed Me to preach… heal the brokenhearted… proclaim liberty to the captives… recovery of sight to the blind… to set at liberty those who are oppressed.* (Luke 4:18) All of these activities are not only described in the anointing of the Spirit "upon" from Isaiah chapter 61, but Isaiah chapter 11, and 2 Chronicles 16:9. This is the full measure equipping providing by all 7 Spirits of the LORD. Remember, Jesus said, *he who believes in Me, the works that I do he will do also; and greater works than these he will do.* (John 14:12)

Why is it important to see that all 7 Spirits were upon Jesus? Because Zechariah described Jesus as the "stone" with the 7 eyes which are the 7 Spirits, and Peter referred to us and Christ as living stones. *Coming to Him as to a living stone, rejected indeed by men, but chosen by God and Precious, you also, as living stones, are being built up a spiritual house, a holy priesthood.* (1 Peter 2:4-5) Therefore we come to Christ as "living stones" having upon us the same "7 eyes" that He has upon Himself. Paul described our bodies as *the temple of the Holy Spirit,* (1 Corinthians 6:19-20) and Peter said that we are "being built up a spiritual house" of living stones, living stones like Christ, which has upon it "7 Eyes." The perspective is that the 7 Spirits are essential for our development and the "let Us make man" original goal and mandate of the LORD.

*That the God of our Lord Jesus Christ, the Father of glory, may give to you the <u>spirit</u> of <u>wisdom</u> **and** <u>revelation</u> in the knowledge of Him, the <u>eyes</u> of your <u>understanding</u> being <u>enlightened</u>; that you may <u>know</u> what is the hope of His calling, what are the riches of the glory of His inheritance in the saints, and what is the exceeding greatness of His power towards us who believe, according to the working of His mighty power which He worked in Christ when He raised Him from the dead.* (Ephesians 1:17-20 emphases added)

The 7 Spirits are essential to our knowing Christ, fully comprehending (seeing/understanding) the hope of His calling, riches of His inheritance, and the greatness of His power towards us who believe. You and I need the 7 Spirits of the LORD upon us, teaching us, counseling us, strengthening us, and making us quick of understanding. The 7 Spirits are part of the Council of God, the "Us" God was referring to when He said, "Let Us make Man." (Genesis 1:26)

In 2011, I had a vision that drastically impacted my life and became the basis of my ministry logo. I saw a flame, and from it came four tongues of fire that formed the shape of a cross. The four ends of the cross, north, south, east, and west, were open with flames flowing out from the four ends. A fifth flame came out of the center of the cross, and formed into the shape of a dove, that rested upon the east extension of the cross. Then I heard a voice saying, "from the crucifixion, flows the power of the resurrection." For this book, I will briefly explain, the revelation of the same Spirit that worked in Christ, now works in you.

It was in this vision that I suddenly knew Christ to a dimension I had never known Him before. This is when the "revelation of Jesus Christ" began to change me into His likeness, as He became revealed to me. (Galatians 1:12, Revelation 1:2, 1 John 3:2)

Jesus, the Son of Man was able to do and accomplish all that he did, through the Spirit that enabled Him. That same Spirit was within and upon me, enabling me to do the same if I would only learn to let Him.

Christ, who through the eternal Spirit offered Himself without spot to God. (Hebrews 9:14) If the same Spirit now lived in me, and He enables Christ to live life as a living sacrifice without spot, He could enable me to do the same.

The Plan Summary

The foundation in God's plan for man resides in His initial statement, *Let Us make man in Our image, according to Our likeness.* (Genesis 1:26) But in order to gain a better understanding of what that means, we have to explore aspects of the image and likeness of the "Us" who God was speaking to. As you progress through this book, you'll see that Jesus Christ is our High Priest and the perfect model (pattern) Son, reflecting God's originally intended plan for man. Jesus, the "perfected captain of our salvation" is the image and likeness God originally planned for man.

We've also come to understand that God planned for every possible attempt to derail His plans. He made provision for man's redemption prior to his falling and need of redemption. He positioned natural and supernatural tutors and governors to guide us through a process of developing His character traits. God is a Strategic Master Planner.

Chapter 2

A Son is Given – (the Pattern Son)

For unto us a Child is born, Unto us a Son is given. (Isaiah 9:6)

The "Child" that was born is the "Son of Man," and the "Son" that was given, is the "Son of God." There is a significant difference between the "Son of Man" and the "Son of God." Jesus often referred to Himself as the Son of Man, which indicates He was attempting to draw attention to His humanity verse His divinity.

In all things He had to be made like His brethren, that He might be a merciful and faithful High Priest in things pertaining to God, to make propitiation for the sins of the people. (Hebrews 2:17) Jesus could not *be a merciful and faithful High Priest* without being made in the likeness of His brethren. That experience of being subjected to everything man is subjected to, gave Him the ability to empathies with man and be moved with compassion. He is intimately acquainted with our sufferings; He knows what you're go through.

Like His brethren, Jesus was vulnerable as a Son of Man, subjected to everything we are subjected to. This may sound blasphemes, but Jesus had the capability of sinning and failing to fulfill the will of God. Some people have a real hard time accepting this as a reality, but consider this, can you be tempted to sin, if it's not even possible to sin. The fact that He *was in all points tempted as we are, yet without sin*, proves that He was capable of sinning. (Hebrews 4:15)

Jesus was fully man and yet He did not fail, He lived His life and remained without spot (blemish). (Hebrews 9:14) And He didn't accomplish this by the virtue of His divinity, He accomplished it in His humanity, through the enabling of the Spirit. Jesus gave us an example, demonstrating that humanity can live in righteousness, without blemish, body, soul, and spirit. (1 Thessalonians 5:23)

For whom He foreknew, He also predestined to be <u>*conformed*</u> *to the* <u>*image*</u> *of His son, that He might be the* <u>*firstborn*</u> *of many brethren.* (Roman 8:29 emphases added)

If Jesus was the firstborn, who are these "many brethren" that are to be born and conformed to His image afterward? Being born and conformed to His image implies that we are His genetic His offspring, having His DNA. *Having been born again, not of corruptible seed but incorruptible, through the word of God which lives and abides forever.* (1 Peter 1:23) The genetics of the Father is passed down to the Son(s).

In Genesis we see the seed principle cited multiple times. *"Let the earth bring forth grass, the herb that yields seed, and the fruit tree that yields fruit according to its kind, whose seed is it itself.* (Genesis 1:11, 12, 21, 24, 28) Everything including man is producing according to its kind. When man was originally created, he was created in the image of God, and was commanded to *be fruitful and multiply*, producing children in the image of God. (Genesis 1:28) However, man did not produce children after the image of God, but after the image of fallen man.

*In the day that God created man, He made him in the likeness of God. He created them male and female, and blessed them and called them Mankind in the day they were created. And Adam lived one hundred and thirty years, and begat a son in **his own likeness**, after his image, and named him Seth.* (Genesis 5:1-3 emphases added)

Adam's failure was that he was no longer able to produce children in the image and likeness of God. He was producing children in his own image and likeness, the image and likeness of a fallen man.

This original commission of reproducing children in the image and likeness of God still exists to this day. It cannot be accomplished through those that born in the image and likeness of the fallen first Adam. This is why we have to be born again after the image and likeness of the last Adam (Jesus). (John 3:3-8, 1 Corinthians 15:45)

We must be born again from the incorruptible seed, after the image and likeness of Christ, offspring according to His kind. And what is His kind? He is a Priest forever, according to the order of Melchizedek, something I'll cover further in the following chapters. (Psalm 110:4)

If Jesus is the Blueprint Pattern Son, and we're supposed to be conformed to His image and likeness, it is essential that we know and understand, what is the full measure of the stature of Christ, the Son of Man.

What is man?

King David was one of a few unique characters in the Bible that held multiple roles. David was a king, priest, and a prophet. David wrote multiple psalms that prophesied future realities and asked significant questions, such as, *"when I consider Your heavens, the works of Your fingers, the moon and the stars, which you have ordained, what is man that You are mindful of him, and the son of man that You visit him?"* (Psalm 8:4 NKJV).

What is so significant about man, that out of everything and everyone in the entire universe; God, granted him dominion, He visits his sons, and even takes time to think about him.

A review of the scriptures will unveil created beings such as seraphim with six wings (Isaiah 6:2), cherubim with four faces and four wings (Ezekiel 1:6), and wheels that had eyes over their entire body (Ezekiel 10:12-13). With these and other magnificently described beings in existence, why does God place so much significance upon man?

Most people would be overwhelmed if they were visited by an angel, yet regarding angels, the Bible says, *"are they not all ministering spirits sent forth to minister for those who will inherit salvation?"* (Hebrews 1:14 NKJV).

In the 8th Psalm David asserts that man has dominion over all the works of God's hands, all things are put under his feet, and man is crowned with glory and honor. To comprehend how David could envision man as having such prominence, I'll address the following statement and questions by highlight that David was a king and priest.

Why did God create you?

What was God's intention when He said, let us make man?

You were predestined to be a king and priest

What is the role and significance of being a king and priest?

What is the process of becoming a king and priest?

Perspective: Unless we have an appropriate perspective of truth, we can make significant decisions that limit or prohibit the full realization of our potential.

By answering the question "why did God create you," we can begin to envision and charter the pathway to the full realization of your God predestined purpose and potential. But how do you see yourself, your significance, your potential, and what do you perceive to be God's perspective of you? How you believe God sees you can significantly limit or prohibit God's plans which is why Jesus said you can make the word of God of no effect (Mark 7:13).

This is clearly demonstrated in the encounter of the twelve spies when *the LORD spoke to Moses, saying, "send men to spy out the land of Canaan, which* ***I am*** *giving to the children of Israel…"* (Numbers 13:1-2) (emphases added)

God, who had just destroyed the most powerful military on earth, sent His word that He was giving them this land. However, their deeply rooted opinions (beliefs/mindset) prevented them from envisioning God's decree as being possible.

The spies sent out were not your average people; God instructed Moses to send out leaders from each tribe (Numbers 13:2). These leaders had significance amongst the people within their tribes, in other words, the people would listen to them and believe them.

The men returned from spying out the land and brought back tangible evidence of the magnificent fruit of the land which included a cluster of grapes requiring two men to carry it on a pole. (Numbers 13:26)

Ten of the twelve spies "gave the children of Israel a bad report of the land." (Numbers 13:30-32) Their report caused the people to doubt that God could give them the land He had promised them. The fact that Caleb had to quieten the people indicates they become fearful and loud. The people become emotional because they now saw themselves through the perspective of the ten spies, a distorted opinion that was opposed to God's perspective."

These ten spies said, *"and we were like grasshoppers in **our sight**, and so we were in **their sight**."* (Numbers 13:33 emphases added) When the LORD had delivered Israel from Egypt's army, they sang saying, *"the people will hear and be afraid; sorrow will take hold of the inhabitants of Philistia. Then the chiefs of Edom will be dismayed; the mighty men of Moab, trembling will take hold* *of them; **all** the **inhabitants** of <u>Canaan</u> will <u>melt away</u>."* (Exodus 15:14-15 emphases added)

Although they had witnessed God's tremendous power and personally declared that "all the inhabitants of Canaan will melt away" trembling in fear, the "bad report" of the ten spies caused them to make the word of God of no effect.

The perspective of others can have a tremendous impact on your own perspective, especially if they are people in positions of influence. Although you may discover "what" and "why" God thinks about you, other's inaccurate perspectives can influence the realization (manifestation) of God's plans (word, purpose, desire).

How does God see you, what has been declared concerning man, and do you believe it?

The Pattern Son Summary

There are two primary points that need to be taken from this section of the book, 1) the Son of God became like us, 2) we are predestined to be conformed to Christ's image. He became like us, and we shall become like Him.

1. *In all things He had to be <u>made like</u> His brethren, that He <u>might be</u> a merciful and faithful High Priest in things pertaining to God, to make propitiation for the sins of the people.* (Hebrews 2:17 emphases added)
2. *For whom He foreknew, He also predestined to be <u>conformed</u> to the <u>image</u>*

of His son, that He might be the firstborn of many brethren. (Roman 8:29 emphases added)

Chapter 3

A Priest Forever – (the Purpose)

D avid's revelation and change in perspective about Christ and the priesthood resulted in his making discoveries and receiving benefits, that no one else during his time experienced.

The LORD has sworn and will not relent, "You are a priest forever according to the order of Melchizedek. (Psalm 110:4)

During this time, the only priesthood that was in operation within Israel was the Levitical Priesthood. Where did David get this priesthood according to the order of Melchizedek and how did it impact his life?

Several of David's activities are associated with priesthood and imply that he functioned as a priest. Not only were these activities prohibited if you were not a priest, but the consequences could also be devastating.

David was clothed with a robe of fine linen, as were all the Levites who bore the ark, the singers, and Chenaniah the music master with the singers. David also wore a linen ephod. (1 Chronicles 15:27)

The wearing of the linen ephod is associated with being a priest of the LORD, as we see described in the book of Samuel. *But the servants of the king would not lift their hands to strike the <u>priest of the LORD</u>. And the king said to Doeg, "You turn and kill the priests!" So Doeg the Edomite turned and <u>struck the priests</u>, and killed on that day eighty-five men who <u>wore a linen ephod</u>.* (1 Samuel 22:17-18 emphases added)

David, however, was not of the tribe of Levi, he was of the tribe of Judah, and to be a priest, you had to be of the tribe of Levi.

The priests, the Levites – all the tribe of Levi…he may serve in the name of the LORD his God as all his brethren the Levites do, who stand there before the Lord. (Deuteronomy 18:1, 7) In the 21st chapter of Leviticus, the LORD specifically identifies the sons of Aaron as those qualified to be priests, if they meet additional requirements. (Leviticus 21) Only those of the tribe of Levi could serve as ministers, and only those born as sons under Aaron could be priests. Any violation of the qualification and consecration requirements could result in death. (Leviticus 8:36, 10:1)

But David, not being a Levi, served as a priest and did not suffer any consequences, how could this be? The answer is within his writing of Psalm 110 about the Priesthood according to the order of Melchizedek. David loved the LORD, and desired something that at the time was only available to the priests, the ability to inquire in the LORD's temple.

One thing I have desired of the LORD, That will I seek: That I may dwell in the house of the LORD All the days of my life, To behold the beauty of the LORD, And to inquire in His temple (Psalm 27:4) David, being a prophet (Acts 2:29-30) saw another priesthood of the LORD according to the order of Melchizedek, through which he and all of us under Christ, would have access into the house of the LORD.

Through faith, David was able to benefit from something fulfilled in eternity, before its manifestation in time. David saw the lamb that was and would be slain (first in eternity than in time), believed, and received the benefit. David saw the Lord seated at the right hand of the LORD and believed. Abraham saw Jesus' day (John 8:56), believed, and it was counted onto him as righteousness (Genesis 15:6, Romans 4:3), even though Jesus at that point had only been slain in eternity and not within time.

Jesus is a priest forever, and if we observe His current activity in heaven, we'll observe that as our High Priest, He *lives to make intercession* for us, a priestly function. (Hebrews 7:25) Jesus, the firstborn of many sons, is a priest, and He is producing sons after His kind, meaning we are supposed to be priests, according to the order of Melchizedek.

The Significance of Melchizedek

For this Melchizedek, king of Salem, <u>priest</u> of the Most High God, who met Abraham returning from the slaughter of the kings and blessed him, to whom also Abraham gave a tenth part of all, first being translated "<u>king of righteousness</u>," and then also king of <u>Salem</u>, meaning "<u>king of peace</u>," without father, without mother, *without genealogy, having neither beginning of days nor end of life, but made like the Son of God, remains a priest continually. Now consider how great this man was...* (Hebrews 7:1-4 emphases added)

David wrote that Jesus was *a priest forever according to the order of Melchizedek.* (Psalm 110:4) If Jesus is a priest according to the order of Melchizedek, this Melchizedek must be extraordinarily great king, and his priesthood extremely significant.

The first thing to recognize is that Melchizedek is a king and a priest. This is significant for believers because according to the writings of Peter and John, we are a *royal priesthood* and are made to be *kings and priests to our God.* (1 Peter 2:9, Revelation 5:10) This confirms that we are following in Jesus' lineage and becoming priests according to the order of Melchizedek.

The name Melchizedek is comprised of two words, malki and tsedeq, malki meaning my king, and tsedeq meaning right or righteousness, my righteous king, or king of righteousness. A Person's name is important because it describes who they are, that's why God changed Abram's name to Abraham because he would no longer be known as an exalted father, but a father of multitudes. (Genesis 17:5)

Melchizedek's name meaning king of righteousness is comparable to the foundation of the LORD's throne, which is righteousness and justice. (Psalm 89:14) And when a king governs in righteousness and justice, peace follows, and Melchizedek happens to be the king of Salem, meaning peace. Peace follows righteous and just governance.

Righteousness and justice are the foundation of Your throne; <u>Mercy</u> and <u>truth</u> go before Your Face. (Psalm 89:14 emphases added) Mercy and truth are provisions brought forth by a priest, which further explains why Melchizedek was not only a king but a priest who makes propitiation and proclaims blessings and truth upon the people. Priests (ministers) functioning in a ministry of reconciliation, proclaim the truth of the Gospel and the blessings of the LORD.

Therefore, if anyone is in Christ, he is a new creation; old things have passed away; behold, all things have become new. Now all things are of God, who has <u>reconciled</u> us to Himself through Jesus Christ, and has given us the <u>ministry of reconciliation</u>. (2 Corinthians 5:17-18 emphases added)

Although we are destined to be kings and priests, the emphasis is not kingship, but priesthood. This is why Paul wrote that God "has given us the ministry of reconciliation," and Jesus is referred to as a "priest forever," not a king forever, although He will forever be King of Kings, priesthood is the emphasis. Priesthood, which is a humble ministry service, a service exemplified by Jesus, who *did not come to be served, but to serve*, is the primary emphases. (Matthew 20:28)

A humble and faithful minister servant can be trusted to rule in righteousness and justice. Jesus became like onto His brethren, subjected to ridicule by those He created, and came not in His own divinity and authority, which are extraordinary acts of obedience, submission, and humility. (Hebrews 2:17, Luke 22:63, John 5:30, 12:49)

Following Jesus' example, we minister as priests governing under the delegated authority, authority for which we'll be held accountable following its use. (Matthew 28:18-19, 25:14-30, Hebrews 13:17)

Priesthood (ministry) Qualifications

When the LORD gave Moses the instructions for building the tabernacle and instituting the Levitical Priesthood, He was very specific and stated, *see to it that you make them according to the pattern which was shown you on the mountain.* (Exodus 25:40) The writer of the book of Hebrews explained that the priesthood instituted by Moses is a *copy and shadow of the heavenly things,* an earthly physical example of that which is in heaven. (Hebrews 8:1-5)

Considering that I have other extensive writings and teachings on the topic of priesthood qualifications, in this book I will only briefly explain the Levitical priesthood qualifications and their spiritual meaning.

The priesthood qualifications are broken down into three categories:

- Maturity
- Birth, or lineage
- Absence of 12 specific blemishes

Although we are not called to be priests under the Levitical Priesthood, this priesthood is a copy and shadow of the heavenly priesthood, and therefore serves as a guide in the priesthood qualification and preparation process.

MATURITY:

Then the LORD spoke to Moses and Aaron, saying: "Take a census of the sons of Kohath from among the children of Levi, by their families, by their fathers' house, from thirty years old and above, even to fifty years old, all who enter the service to do the work in the tabernacle of meeting. (Numbers 4:1-3)

Age referred to maturity, and the age of maturity was classified as thirty years of age. Jesus would become a priest according to the heavenly priesthood after the order of Melchizedek, not the Levitical Priesthood. However, being that the Levitical Priesthood was a copy and shadow of the heavenly priesthood, Jesus did not begin his ministry until he met the maturity requirement.

Now Jesus Himself began His ministry at about thirty years of age… (Luke 3:23) Until He fulfilled the maturity requirement classified as 30 years of age, Jesus did not begin His ministry. Maturity signifies that the child has completed the tutoring and governing timeline established by the father.

Now I say, That the heir, as long as he is a child, differeth nothing from a servant, though he be lord of all; But is under tutors and governors until the time appointed of the father…But when the fullness of the time was come, God sent forth his Son…that we might receive the adoption of sons…wherefore thou art no more a servant, but a son; and if a son, then an heir of God through Christ. (Galatians 4:1-7 KJV)

In the letter to the Galatians, Paul illustrates that we and Jesus are heirs, and that heirs are placed under tutors and governors until the appointed time. The father does not send out a son until the fullness of the time has come.

BIRTH:

The LORD had spoken to Moses, saying…you shall appoint the Levites over the <u>*tabernacle of the Testimony*</u>*, over all its* <u>*furnishings*</u>*, and over all* <u>*things*</u> *that belong to it…when the tabernacle is to go forward, the Levites shall* <u>*take it down*</u>*; and when the tabernacle is to be set up, the Levites shall* <u>*set it up*</u>*. The outsider who comes near shall be* <u>*put to death*</u>*.* (Numbers 1:47-48, 50-51 emphases added)

The Levites were appointed the responsibility of attending to the tabernacle, the furnishings, setting it up, taking it down, and moving it when it was time to move. The Levites ministered (attended) to the needs of Aaron, his sons, the congregation before the tabernacle of meeting, and the children of Israel, but they did not minister to the LORD as priests.

And these are the names of the sons of Aaron: Nadab, the firstborn, and Abihu, Eleazar, and Ithamar. These are the names of the sons of Aaron, the <u>*anointed priests*</u>*, Nadab and Abihu had died before the LORD when they offered profane fire before the LORD in the Wilderness of Sinai; and they had no children. So Eleazar and Ithamar* <u>*ministered as priests*</u> *in the presence of Aaron their father.* (Numbers 3:1-4 emphases added)

The sons of Aaron are specifically identified as being anointed and ministering as priest.

And the LORD spoke to Moses, saying: "Bring the tribe of Levi near, and present them before Aaron the priest, that they may <u>serve him</u>. And they shall <u>attend</u> to <u>his needs</u> and the needs of the <u>whole congregation</u> before the tabernacle of meeting, to do the work of the tabernacle. Also they shall attend to all the furnishings of the tabernacle of meeting, and to the <u>needs</u> of the <u>children of Israel</u>, to do the <u>work of the tabernacle</u>. And you shall give the Levites to Aaron and his sons, they are given entirely to him from among the children of Israel. So you shall <u>appoint Aaron</u> and his <u>sons</u>, and <u>they shall attend to their priesthood</u>; but the outsider who comes near shall be put to death." (Numbers 3:5-10 emphases added)

The Levites are given to Aaron and his sons for the "work of the tabernacle," but not the priesthood. Only Aaron and his sons are appointed to serve as priests. This is reflective of how believers can be a part of the tribe of Levi, and do the ministry work of the tabernacle, ministering to the people, but not qualify to minister as priests. This refers to birth within the Levi tribe, but not under the Aaron the High Priest. This is illustrated in the conversation Jesus had with Nicodemus when He explained that you must be born again to "see" the kingdom and born of the water and spirit to "enter." (John 3:1-21)

In the parable of the ten virgins, their virginity symbolizes purity through the blood of Christ, and their lamps symbolize that Christ had lit their lights which He had not intended to be hidden. (Luke 11:33) In the end, the bridegroom said to them "I do not know you," and they were shutout in the outer court. (Matthew 25:1-30, 8:12) It is possible to be a Levite ministering in and around the tabernacle, and never enter the Holy of Holies as a priest.

BLEMISHES:

When the LORD identified these 12 blemishes that a priest could not have, He was not discriminating against individuals because of physical blemishes. He was demonstrating a spiritual attribute through a physical illustration that would be essential in the heavenly priesthood. (Leviticus 21:16-24) These physical blemishes are intended to point out a spiritual flaw illustrated through a physical flaw.

In reviewing these physical blemishes, consider what they represent from the perspective of a spiritual blemish that a heavenly priest cannot possess.

God used physical illustrations man could see and understand, that would subsequently be related to spiritual truths man needed to comprehend.

Mankind had lost its ability to see, communicate, and understand in the spiritual realm. Therefore, God began to teach man truths through natural things, so that he would subsequently understand spiritual truths hidden within natural illustrations.

Teachings such as "eyes to see but does not see, and ears to hear but does not hear" were understood to mean more than natural seeing and hearing. (Ezekiel 12:2, Jeremiah 5:21, Matthew 3:13)

BLINDNESS:

o be blind means to have no vision or ability to see what the Father is doing or desiring to do. In speaking with Nicodemus, Jesus said, *Most assuredly, I say to you, unless one is born again, he* cannot <u>see</u> *the kingdom of God.* (John 3:3 emphases added) A man cannot enter the kingdom of God unless he can see, and he cannot see unless he is born again. To inherit the kingdom a man must enter, and he cannot enter and inherit what he cannot see.

Can the blind lead the blind? Will they not both fall into the ditch? (Luke 6:39)

LAMENESS:

A spiritually lame man cannot walk out the truths that are being revealed by Holy Spirit. A spiritually lame person may be able to see, but he cannot manifest the truth or spiritual reality being revealed. This is reflected in the fig tree that had leaves but no fruit. (Mark 11:12-14) A fig tree that has leaves should at minimum have something called taqsh, which are small knobs that can be eaten.

In the story of the fig tree that withered, Jesus cursed the tree because it was portraying that it had fruit for nourishment when in fact it did not. (Mark 11:12-14) It's like *having a form of godliness but denying its power…from such people turn away!* (2 Timothy 3:5)

FLAT NOSE:

The nose is the instrument of discernment. The nose is our sensory organ that smell the aroma to discern if it is fresh, rotten, pure, or defiled. Based upon experience and highly sensitive toxic warning sensory, the nose can rapidly identify the aroma of a substance and alert the brain of the benefit or detriment it poses to the body.

The nose is the first part of the body that contacted the life-given breath of God. (Genesis 2:7) *The Spirit of God has made me, And the breath of the Almighty gives me life.* (Job 33:4 emphases added)

The nose (sensory of smell) is the instrument of spiritual discernment, which is why people say, "Something just doesn't smell right about this." If the nose is defective, it's sense of smell (discernment) will be flawed and could result in exposure to toxic fumes.

SUPERFLUOUS (LIMB TOO LONG):

The Hebrew word for superfluous is "sara" which means to prolong, extend, overgrown, for example; to be deformed, be excess of members…adding to the body; six toes, fingers, etc.

Examples of superfluous include exaggeration, aggrandizement, and perversion. When the disciples were not able to cast out a demon, Jesus said to them, *O faithless and perverse generation, how long shall I be with you and bear with you?* (Luke 9:41, Matthew 17:14-21) A deeper study of this teaching reveals that the perverted beliefs of the disciples had affected their faith, a perverted traditional mindset that could make the word of God of no effect. (Mark 7:13)

To be superfluous means something that's been altered from its original course, meaning, or state, to a distortion or corruption of what was initially intended, such as the creation of Nephilim (giants) through an unholy union (paganism). (Genesis 6:1-4)

BROKEN FOOT:

A man with a Broken Foot is a man with a weak or weakened foundation, his foundation has been damaged (injured), or it was never properly fashioned to a solid Anchor Point, a secure Corner Stone.

A man with a Broken Foot has no ROOT within himself, he has a stony heart that holds onto unforgiveness, and it weakens his foundation, he can only endure for a short season, but when tribulation or persecution arises because of the word, he stumbles. The parable of the sower, and of the wise man who built his house on the rock, illustrate the need for a strong foundation. (Matthew 7:24-27, 13:1-23)

BROKEN HAND:

The hand represents the outer actions, service, strength, and ministry. The hand is the servant member of the body. A body with a broken hand becomes vulnerable and struggles to sustain itself. Instead of ministering to the needs of others, it has to be ministered to.

Fear not, for I am with you; Be not dismayed, for I am your God. I will strengthen you, Yes, I will help you, I will uphold you with My righteous right hand. (Isaiah 41:10)

CROOKBACK (HUNCHBACK):

A man with a crookback represents a weak backbone, his ability to stand strong under pressure is severely compromised, he cannot weather the storms of life.

That we should no longer be children, tossed to and fro and carried about with every wind of doctrine, by the trickery of men, in the cunning craftiness of deceitful plotting. (Ephesians 4:14)

DWARFISM:

The man with dwarfism is one that never fully grows to produce fruit in accordance with the incorruptible seed and does not multiply the originally given talent. (Matthew 25:14-30) He is *always learning and never able to come to the knowledge of the truth.* (2 Timothy 3:7)

He also spoke this parable: "A certain man had a fig tree planted in his vineyard, and he came seeking fruit on it and found none, 'Look, for three years I have come seeking fruit on this fig tree and find none. Cut it down; why does it use up the ground?' But he answered and said to him, 'Sir, let it alone this year also, until I dig around it and fertilize it. And if it bears fruit, well. But if not, after that you can cut it down!" (Luke 13:6-9)

DEFECT IN THE EYE:

The eye is the figure of knowledge and understanding, the lamp that illuminates the body, if the eye is defective, the illumination will also be defective (Matthew 6:22-24)

A blemish in the eye speaks of an impaired vision, something blocking or hindering the viewing of the full truth and reality of God.

That the God of our Lord Jesus Christ, the Father of glory, may give to you the spirit wisdom and revelation in the knowledge of Him, the eyes of your understanding being enlightened; that you may know what is the hope of His calling, what are the riches of the glory of His inheritance in the saints. (Ephesians 1:17-18)

ECZEMA (SCURVY):

Eczema (Scurvy) is a sickness that is caused by not eating an important food element called Vitamin C. It is an outward manifestation of an internal deficiency, an insufficiently balanced diet. The underlying cause of the sickness has to be discovered to be corrected. This is a carnal mind based upon inappropriate teaching and traditions of men, such as the leaven of the Pharisees. (Mark 7:13, Matthew 16:6)

My son, give attention to my words; incline your ear to my sayings. Do not let them depart from your ears; Keep them in the midst of your heart; For they are life to those who find them, And health to all their flesh. Keep your heart with all diligence, For out of it spring the issues of life. (Proverbs 4:20-23)

If these appropriate teachings are life and bring health, then inappropriate teaching brings sickness and death. This is why the renewing of the mind is essential.

SCABS AND OPEN SORES:

In the New International Version of the Bible this is called "running or festering sores." It is an inward uncleanness that erupts in the outward discharge of pus.

This speaks of inward uncleanness of impure thoughts, motives, and desires which erupt into the outward manifestation by unholy conduct.

They are spots and blemishes, carousing in their own deceptions while they feast with you, having eyes full of adultery and that cannot cease from sin, enticing unstable souls. They have a heart trained in covetous practices, and are accursed children. They have forsaken the right way and gone astray, following the way of Balaam the son of Beor, who loved the wages of unrighteousness. (2 Peter 2:13-15)

BROKEN STONES (EUNUCH):

The stones are the reproductive glands in a man's body. A man with broken stones cannot produce life, he cannot reproduce, he cannot bring forth sons in the image and likeness of God.

Man was significant in that he could reproduce sons in the image and likeness of God. Adam's original mandate was to *be fruitful and multiply*, produce children in the image and likeness of God. This mandate remains to this day, which is why Jesus said *make disciples of all the nations.*

(Genesis 1:28, Matthew 28:19-20)

For whom He foreknew, He also predestined to be conformed to the image of His Son, that He might be the <u>firstborn</u> among <u>many brethren</u>. (Romans 8:29 emphases added)

A priest that has any of these blemishes is lacking attributes necessary for equipping and edifying the saints, and may infect others with their blemishes.

This is why sanctification is essential, the washing with the word, sanctification with the truth, the revelation of Jesus Christ. (Exodus 30:17-19, Ephesians 5:26, John 17:17)

Tabernacle Pattern and Priesthood Hidden Meanings

When we observe the Tabernacle of Moses, we need to consider that it is a copy of and shadow, of a heavenly sanctuary erected by the Lord, and everything within it has symbolic meaning, hidden mysteries waiting to be unveiled.

For this book, I will only highlight a few aspects of the tabernacle that illustrate the overall goal of "Let Us make man" in God's original mandate.

THE PERFECTED PRIEST:

*For it was fitting for Him, for whom are all things and by whom are all things, in bringing many sons to glory, to <u>make</u> the <u>captain of their salvation</u> **perfect** through <u>sufferings</u> For both He who sanctifies and those who are being sanctified are all of one, for which reason He is not ashamed to call them brethren.* (Hebrews 2:10-11 emphases added)

The key points I want to highlight in this scripture are:

- Make; completed at the end of a process, progressing from a condition of not being made, to a condition of being made.
- Jesus, the Son of Man (in His humanity), was not yet perfect but was made perfect.
- Perfection was accomplished when Christ stepped into His role as the High Priest to make the propitiation for our sin.

Jesus Christ, the Captain of our Salvation was perfected at the culmination of the crucifixion, what does this mean? It means that PERFECTION was accomplished at the climax of the crucifixion when Christ stepped into His role as the High Priest making propitiation for our sins. Having been perfected, He remains a priest forever.

The relevance is that when Christ stepped into the FULLNESS of His priesthood as our High Priest presenting the sacrifice, His PERFECTION was accomplished. The FULLNESS of Priesthood is the reflection of PERFECTION. Any ministry operation outside of priesthood perfection is imperfection and blemished.

When we observe the priesthood process, the Tabernacle, and its furnishings, we need to understand that everything is concealing mysteries of the Priesthood Perfection. God's ultimate plan was to make sons in His image and likeness as kings and priests according to the order of Melchizedek.

THE TABERNACLE AND ITS FURNISHINGS:

The reason that the LORD told Moses, *see to it that you make them according to the pattern which was shown you on the mountain*, was so that it would function as a testimony of the LORD's ultimate intention, making sons in the **"fullness of priesthood perfection**,*"* which in the fullness of the measure of the stature of Christ.

OFFERINGS AT THE BRONZE ALTAR: This is the point at which reconciliation is accomplished, granting access to proceed in the process of sanctification, enlightenment, regeneration, ascension, and transfiguration/glorification.

WASHING AT THE BRONZE LAVER: This is the washing of the word, the sanctification by His truth which is His word, a renewing of the mind, until you see things appropriately, beholding as is a mirror the glory of the Lord. (Exodus 38:8, 2 Corinthians 3:18) Washing the hands and feet pertain to your walk and your work/ministry.

GOLDEN LAMPSTAND: The illumination or enlightenment of the eyes of our heart/understanding. These symbolize the 7 Spirits of the LORD, and the angels of the churches bring enlightenment of the word.

TABLE OF SHOWBREAD: Symbolizes reclining and fellowship in communion with the manna of regeneration bring us into unified oneness, the unity of the faith.

ALTAR OF INCENSE: Spiritual prayer, worship, and transformation resulting in an ascension into the heavenly places which include going beyond the veil into the Most Holy Place.

THE VEIL: Is that which prevents us from entering into the Most Holy Place, the law enacted because of sin and death. The removing of the veil of the consciousness of sin and death resulting in admission and ascension into the Most Holy Place.

THE ARK OF THE COVENANT AND THE MERCY SEAT: The ark is a mobile transportation sanctuary upon which the glory of the LORD rests and dwells. It symbolizes man within whom is the testimony, manna, restored authoritative resurrection staff, upon which the priestly mercy seat rests. The transfiguration and manifestation of the glorified Christ in you.

The Purpose Summary

Jesus is the perfect man and pattern (model) Son. In the conclusion of His life and ministry on earth, He finished the work when He stepped into His ministry function as the sacrificial Lamb and High Priest. As our High Priest, He brought the spotless sacrifice to the Father as the propitiation for our sins. Jesus was perfected at the moment He became our High Priest, and He remains a priest forever, according to the order of Melchizedek.

The priesthood according to the order of Melchizedek is a Royal Priesthood which is Kingly and Priestly, Governance Authority and Merciful Grace. A Royal Priest rules in righteousness and justice and is identified by love, mercy, and peace.

Whenever someone come to the fullness (full revelation, transformation, and transfiguration) of the Priesthood Perfection, they have come to the full image and likeness God originally intended, the measure of the stature of the fullness of Christ.

Chapter 4

A Renewed Perspective – (the Process)

As a child, my dad would often trick me with this question; "How do you see it? (he would momentarily pause for an answer) and right before I answered, he would say, "with your eyes." As we grew up, my brother and I would pull the same trick on each other.

Although my dad played this trick pretending to be asking for our perspective on a subject, I genuinely ask you, how do you see it?

Referring to the people of His day, Jesus explained that the Isaiah was correct when he stated, *I speak to them in parables, because seeing they do not see, and hearing they do not hear, nor do they understand.* (Matthew 13:13-15, Isaiah 6:9-10)

How is it that someone can see and yet not see? In an attempt to explain this, I will utilize a comparison of Light verse Darkness, Day verse Night, and Accurate Information (Truth) verse Inaccurate Information (Lies, Misinformation, and Deception).

Here is another scenario in which an article of furniture in the tabernacle comes into play. The veil prevented everyone from seeing into the Most Holy Place. This is similar to when Jesus said that you must be born again to simply SEE the kingdom of God. (John 3:3) Paul also wrote, *but their minds were blinded. For until this day the same veil remains unlifted in the reading of the Old Testament... But even to this day, when Moses is read, a veil lies on their heart.* (2 Corinthians 3:15) The act of turning to Jesus removes the veil, which initiates the process of restoring a proper perspective, a renewing of your perspective and way of thinking (renewing of your mind). (2 Corinthians 3:16, Romans 12:2, Ephesians 4:23)

The further we study the topic of seeing; we'll recognize that there are various aspects of vision that translate as differing perspectives. What differentiates one perspective from another is the illumination or light source, which we'll eventually identify as being Light or Darkness. For simplicity purposes, consider that Darkness impedes visibility, while Light enhances it. Therefore, if you are walking in the Darkness (Night), your walk may go off the path with stumbling experiences, but when Light begins to be introduced, your walking experience begins to improve, as your walk progresses into the Day.

Day and Night, or Light and Darkness, are referring to being of a specific school of thinking, customs, or standard of living. This is how the traditions of men whose thinking is following Darkness, can make the word of God (customs of Light), of no effect, it's a dark overcast blocking out light.

Consider these day and light scriptures referring to believers:

Jesus answered, "Are there not twelve hours in the day? If anyone walks in the day, he does not stumble, because he sees the light of this world. (John 11:9)

You are all sons of light and sons of the day. We are not of the night nor of darkness. (1 Thessalonians 5:5)

Every good gift and every perfect gift is from above, and comes down from the Father of lights, with whom there is no variation or shadow of turning. (James 1:17)

Saul, later known as Paul, had a distorted perspective until he saw the light that temporarily blinded his eyes, his old method of seeing. These are analogies of a physical experience, but it's interesting how the Lord changed his perspective (method of seeing things) through an encounter with Light, that temporarily blinded him. This is simply an illustration of how an encounter with light, can change someone's darkened perspective.

Are there any schools of thought, customs, or standards of living we possess, that may be influenced or distorted by darkened counsel of words without knowledge? (Job 38:2)

The Light within you (good or bad)

"No one, when he has <u>lit</u> a <u>lamp</u>, puts it in a secret place or under a basket, but on a lampstand, that those who <u>come in</u> may <u>see</u> the <u>light</u>. The <u>lamp</u> of the <u>body</u> is the <u>eye</u>. Therefore, when your eye is <u>good</u>, your <u>whole</u> body also is <u>full</u> of <u>light</u>. But

when your eye is <u>bad</u>, your body also is <u>full</u> of <u>darkness</u>. Therefore <u>take heed</u> that the **<u>light</u>** *which is in you is <u>not</u>* **<u>darkness</u>**. (Luke 11:33-35 emphases added)

The primary points I will highlight in this scripture are that the eye is the illuminator of the whole body, and that light and darkness are both referred to as being light, which can be categorized as opposing illumination sources.

DARKNESS ILLUMINATION VS LIGHT ILLUMINATION:

Jesus refers to the darkness as light; "take heed that the **light** which is in you is not **darkness**." How can darkness be light? This indicates that darkness and light are something beyond what our minds want to envision, such as natural sunlight of the day and darkness of the night.

We know that light illuminates, and if Darkness is referred to as a light source, then it is reasonable that Darkness Light also illuminates. The source or quality of the illumination determines the extent of visibility, which directly impacts perspective.

For now we are looking in a mirror that gives only a dim (blurred) reflection [of reality as in a riddle or enigma], but then [when perfection comes] we shall see in reality and face to face! Now I know in part (imperfectly), but then I shall know and understand fully and clearly, even in the same manner as I have been fully and clearly known and understood [by God]. (1 Corinthians 13:12 AMPCE)

But we all, with unveiled face, beholding as in a mirror the glory of the Lord, are being transformed into the same image from glory to glory, just as by the Spirit of the Lord. (2 Corinthians 3:18)

As illustrated in these two scriptures, darkness veils (obstructs) our ability to see clearly the reflection in the mirror. But when the veil of darkness (lies, misinformation, and deception) is removed, we see clearly, and behold "the glory of the Lord." The consequences of the revealing (revelation) of the Lord are significant; for *we know that when He is revealed, we shall be like Him, for we shall see Him as He is.* (1 John 3:2)

Light illuminates in the DAY and Darkness illuminates in the NIGHT, this is what I have already alluded to regarding Day and Night. It's what I call the "Day and Night Affect," those influenced by teaching, traditions, and customs of the Day, walk in the Light, and children of the Night, walk in Darkness.

THE FULLNESS OF LIGHT OR DARKNESS:

The lamp of the body is the eye. Therefore, when your eye is good, your <u>whole body</u> also is full of light. But when your eye is bad, your body also is <u>full</u> of darkness. (Luke 11:34 emphases added)

The extent to which the eye is either good or bad determines the extent to which the body is filled with light or darkness. This is why good people can still do evil things because they have members of their bodies filled with darkness. The greater the extent of darkness, the greater the extent of evil. The reason God flooded the earth was because *every intent of the thoughts of the heart was only evil continually.* (Genesis 6:5) The more a person's perspective becomes darkened, their behavior will be evil more consistently, with greater depths of wickedness.

Is the light within you Light or Darkness, good or bad, accurate or inaccurate teachings, customs, and/or traditions? Throughout our lives, we've been exposed to both accurate and inaccurate teachings that have formed our beliefs.

Teachings and Traditions of Pharisees

Then Jesus said to them, "Take heed and beware of the leaven of the Pharisees and the Sadducees" ...And they reasoned among themselves, saying, "It is because we have taken no bread" ... How is it you do not understand that I did not speak to you concerning bread? but to beware of the leaven of the Pharisees and Sadducees." Then they understood that He did not tell them to beware of the leaven of bread, but of the doctrine of the Pharisees and Sadducees. (Matthew 16:6-12)

The warning was concerning teachings that could cause the recipients to develop inappropriate beliefs and expectations with devastating consequences. Deeply ingrained inaccurate perspectives could motivate someone like Saul (the future apostle Paul) to become a fierce oppositional enemy of Truth.

An inaccurate expectation concerning the coming of the messiah, caused Peter to oppose the actual messiah, and attempt to overturn the will, plan, and purpose of God.

Jesus asked His disciples, saying, "Who do men say that I, the Son of Man, am?" So they said, "Some say John the Baptist, some Elijah, and others Jeremiah or one of the prophets." (Matthew 16:13-14)

The fact that there were so many opinions of who Jesus was, illustrates the extent of inaccurate information about Christ that was being circulated.

Jesus then asked them, *"But who do you say that I am?"* Simon Peter answered and said, *"You are the Christ, the Son of the living God." Jesus answered and said to him, "Blessed are you, Simon Bar-Jonah, for flesh and blood has not revealed this to you, but My Father who is in heaven.* (Matthew 16:15-17)

Peter, in a moment of spiritual revelation, accurately declares who Jesus is. Jesus compliments Peter for having received this revelation from the Father in heaven.

From that time Jesus began to show to His disciples that He must go to Jerusalem, and suffer many things from the elders and chief priests and scribes, and be killed, and be raised the third day. (Matthew 16:21)

However, Peter, having a preconceived expectation that the Messiah would deliver the Jews from their oppressors, and reign as king forever, would not stand for any talk of the Messiah being killed. Remember, even the people said to Christ, *We have heard from the law that the Christ remains forever; and how can You say, 'The Son of Man must be lifted up'?* (John 12:34)

*Then Peter took Him aside and began to <u>rebuke</u> Him, saying, "Far be it from You, Lord; **this shall not happen** to You!" But He [Jesus] turned and said to Peter, "Get behind Me, Satan! You are an <u>offense to Me</u>, for you are not <u>mindful</u> of* the *things of God, but the things of men.*" (Matthew 16:22-23 emphases added)

This same Peter, who had just been complimented for his revelation, suddenly became an offense to Christ, because of an inaccurate mindset. The name Satan means adversary, and Peter suddenly found himself in alignment with the forces of darkness, an adversary to the truth and purpose of God. He was an offense to Jesus not only because of that opposition but because his close relationship could tug on Jesus' heart. Those that are the closest to you, have the greatest influence and capability of motivating disobedience.

In all of our devoted sincerity, an inaccurate perspective and expectation can cause us to become an offense and adversary to God.

Guard your Heart

I've always found it interesting that when God flooded the earth, the main reason for doing so wasn't because of the sinful activity of the people, but because *every intent of the thoughts of his* [man's] *heart was evil continually.* (Genesis 6:5). All good and evil ultimately come from the heart, and if the heart is completely filled with darkness, from it will flow evil continually.

Above all else, guard your heart, for everything you do flows from it. (Proverbs 4:23 NIV)

Proverbs 4:23 is illustrating to us that everything you do is based upon the condition of your heart. If your heart is healthy then healthy things come out of it. But if it is unhealthy, then unhealthy things come out of it.

For as he thinks in his heart, so is he, "eat and drink!" he says to you, But his heart is not with you. (Proverbs 23:7)

But those things which proceed out of the mouth <u>come from the heart</u>, and they defile a man. For out of the heart proceed <u>evil</u> thoughts, murders, adulteries, fornications, thefts, false witness, blasphemies. These are the things which defile a man. (Matthew 15:18-20 emphases added)

Both good and evil and evil ultimately find their origin in the heart, therefore the soil of the heart must be guarded above all else.

In the parable of the sower, (Matthew 13:1-9, 18-23) Jesus explained that the sower had sown seeds in four types of soil. He later explained that the "seed" was the "word of the kingdom" and the four types of soil are four variations of the condition of a person's heart.

The seeds can represent the word of the kingdom of God, or the tares sown by the enemy. (Matthew 13:25) The point is that there are both good and bad seeds being sown in the soil of men's hearts.

Based upon the condition of the soil (heart) and the quality of the seeds sown, the produce will be either nothing, thirty, sixty, or a hundredfold. With this enhanced understanding, it is incumbent upon us to till the soil of our heart, skillfully remove any evil seeds or tares, and regulate the seeds that are planted and watered.

The Power of Seeing

Beloved, now we are children of God; and it has not yet been revealed <u>what we shall</u> *<u>be</u>, but we know that when He is <u>revealed</u>, we shall **be like Him**, for we shall **see*** *Him as He is. And everyone who has this hope in Him <u>purifies himself</u>, just as He* *is pure... Whoever sins has neither **seen** Him nor **known** Him...And by this we* *know that we <u>are of</u> the **truth**, and shall assure our <u>hearts</u> before Him.* (1 John 3:2-3,6, 19 emphases added)

Seeing the Light of Christ, which is truth, will have a tremendous impact on us as a whole (body, soul, spirit). In this scripture, John is testifying that we "are" children of God, but we still don't know what we shall be. Why, because Christ has not been fully revealed. Once Christ is revealed and we SEE Him "as He is," we become like Him.

We become like Christ to the extent He's been revealed.

We've been instructed to be Christlike, and to a certain extent, we have been developing Christlike character traits. (1 Corinthians 4:16, Ephesians 5:1-2) If we can't be like Him unless He is revealed to us, then he would have to be revealed, so that we can become like Him. Otherwise, it would be unfair to instruct us to be like Him, if He is not being revealed.

However, we are only changed to the extent Christ is revealed, which is why we still possess flawed character traits. This is reflected in the father that said to Jesus, *Lord, I believe; help my unbelief!* (Mark 9:24) Belief had developed to the extent he could see, and he needed help to believe to the extent he could not see.

Although we have only seen in part, the scriptures are clear, in the last days, knowledge shall increase. (Daniel 12:4)

Chapter 5

Arise and Shine – (the Manifestation)

Arise, shine;

For your <u>light</u> **has come**!

And the <u>glory</u> of the Lord **is** risen upon you.

For behold, the <u>darkness</u> shall cover the earth,

And <u>deep darkness</u> the **people**;

But the Lord will arise <u>over you</u>,

And <u>His glory</u> will be <u>seen</u> upon you.

The Gentiles shall come to **your light**,

And kings to the <u>brightness</u> of <u>your rising</u>. (Isaiah 60:1-3 emphases added)

When Isaiah said "for your light has come" he was referring to the light of Christ. (John 1:1-9)

In His prayer to the Father, Jesus prayed, *glorify Me together with Yourself, with the <u>glory</u> which I had with You <u>before</u> the world was.* (John 17:5 emphases added) *And the <u>glory</u> which You <u>gave Me</u> I <u>have given them</u>, that they may be one just as We are one: I in them, and You in Me; that they may be <u>made perfect</u> in one.* (John 17:22-23)

The Lord has given you the same glory the Father gave Him, the glory He had with the Father before the world was. Imagine your significance to the Lord, that He gave you that same glory.

Although darkness may cover the earth, and deep darkness is overshadowing the people, the glory of the Lord has risen upon you. The magnificence of His truth, enlightening the eyes of your understanding, will be a beacon of light to the people of the world. Rulers, governors, and kings will be drawn to the brightness of your rising, like the brightness of Solomon's wisdom that attracted rulers from around the world. (1 Kings 10:1-13)

All of creation has been waiting, for the moment you would enter the fullness of priesthood perfection, to the measure of the stature of the fullness of Christ, the manifestation of the sons of God. (Romans 8:19, Ephesians 4:13)

The time has come, for you to Arise, and Shine!

Initiating the process towards manifestation

With an enhanced understanding of the "let Us make man" goal, we can initiate practices that aid progression through the priesthood perfection process.

It all begins with discipleship, which is why Jesus instructed to *make disciples of all the nations… teaching them to observe all things that I have commanded you.* (Matthew 28:19-20) A disciple is exemplified by consistent discipline, which results in being assigned trusted responsibilities. Eventually, the faithful disciple transitions to the status of an entrusted friend and a consecrated, authorized, and empowered Priest-King.

The following are a few recommendations for the training of a disciple, and development of a son:

This Book of the Law shall not depart from your mouth, but you shall <u>meditate</u> in it day and night, that you may <u>observe</u> to do according to all that is written in it. For <u>then</u> you will <u>make</u> your way <u>prosperous</u>, and then you will <u>have</u> good <u>success</u>. (Joshua 1:8 emphases added)

Finally, brethren, whatever things are <u>true</u>, whatever things are <u>noble</u>, whatever things are <u>just</u>, whatever things are <u>pure</u>, whatever things are <u>lovely</u>, whatever things are of <u>good report</u>, if there is <u>any virtue</u> and if there is anything <u>praiseworthy</u>, <u>__meditate__</u> on these things. (Philippians 4:8 emphases added)

Develop the habit of meditating on the things of God, on His word which has the ability to sanctify our minds of darkened counsel and leading us on the pathway illuminated by the Light of the Day.

- Pray the Ephesians 1:17-23 prayer EVERY day for a minimum of six months, preferably indefinitely.

I have slightly rewritten the Amplified Bible, Classic Edition version of the Ephesians 1 prayer. Read this rewritten first-person version of the prayer as if it were your own personal prayer. While reading this prayer, be asking the Lord to give you a complete understanding of all its individual components. (The strikethrough words have been replaced with a personal words so you can pray it as your own personal prayer)

¹⁷ *[For I always pray to] the God of* **my** ~~our~~ *Lord Jesus Christ, the Father of glory, that* **You** ~~He~~ *may grant* **me** ~~you~~ *a spirit of wisdom and revelation [of insight into mysteries and secrets] in the [deep and intimate]* **knowledge of Him**,

¹⁸ *By having the eyes of* **my** ~~your~~ *heart flooded with light, so that* **I** ~~you~~ *can know and understand the hope to which He has called* **me** ~~you~~, *and how rich is His glorious inheritance in the saints (His set-apart ones),*

¹⁹ *And [so that* **I** ~~you~~ *can know and understand] what is the immeasurable and unlimited and surpassing greatness of His power in and for us who believe, as demonstrated in the working of His mighty strength,*

²⁰ *Which He exerted in Christ when He raised Him from the dead and seated Him at His [own] right hand in the heavenly [places],*

²¹ *Far above all rule and authority and power and dominion and every name that is named [above every title that can be conferred], not only in this age and in this world, but also in the age and the world which are to come.*

²² *And He has put all things under His feet and has appointed Him the universal and supreme Head of the church [a headship exercised throughout the church],*

²³ *Which* **is** *His body, the* **fullness** *of Him Who fills all in all [for in that body lives the* **full measure** *of Him Who makes everything complete, and Who fills everything everywhere with Himself].* (Ephesians 1:17-23 AMPCE emphases added and changes annotated with line strikethrough)

After completing this prayer, read the below-listed scriptures following the day of the week. Read these scriptures for at least four (4) weeks, at which point you can select another scripture to replace these daily reading and meditating verses. The scriptures selected should always be short (1-3 verses) and relate to something for which you're seeking greater insight. (Matthew 13:11)

When you have completed the daily **Ephesians 1** prayer and read the selected scripture, take approximately 5-minutes to meditate (ponder, think upon) the prayer and/or scripture, while softly praying out loud in the spirit. If you happen to have never prayed in the spirit, below is an exercise you can follow to enhance your ability to hear in the spirit.

MONDAY SCRIPTURE:

*⁹ Do not lie to one another, since you have put off the <u>old man</u> with his deeds, ¹⁰ and have put on the <u>new man</u> who is <u>renewed</u> **in knowledge** <u>according</u> to the <u>image</u> of Him who created him.* (Colossians 3:9-10 emphases added)

TUESDAY SCRIPTURE:

⁶ and raised us up <u>together</u>, and made us <u>sit</u> together in the <u>heavenly</u> <u>places</u> in Christ Jesus. (Ephesians 2:6 emphases added)

WEDNESDAY SCRIPTURE:

*² Beloved, <u>now</u> we are <u>children of God</u>; and it has <u>not yet</u> been <u>revealed</u> what we shall be, but we know that <u>when</u> He is **revealed**, we <u>shall</u> be **like Him**, for we shall <u>see</u> Him <u>as He is</u>.* (1 John 3:2 emphases added)

THURSDAY SCRIPTURE:

*¹⁷ that Christ may dwell in your hearts through faith; that you, being <u>rooted</u> and grounded in **<u>love</u>**, ¹⁸ may be able to <u>comprehend</u> with all the saints what is the **<u>width</u>** and **<u>length</u>** and **<u>depth</u>** and **<u>height</u>** ¹⁹ to <u>know</u> the <u>love of Christ</u> which passes knowledge; that you may be <u>filled</u> with all the <u>fullness</u> of God.* (Ephesians 3:17-19 emphases added)

FRIDAY SCRIPTURE:

*⁹ I am the **<u>door</u>**. If anyone <u>enters</u> by Me, he will be saved, and <u>will go</u> **in** <u>and</u> **out** and find <u>pasture</u>.* (John 10:9 emphases added)

SATURDAY SCRIPTURE:

¹⁷ Love has been <u>perfected</u> among us in this: that we may have boldness in the day of judgment; because <u>as He is</u>, <u>so are we</u> in this world. (1 John 4:17 emphases added)

SUNDAY SCRIPTURE:

*²³ Now may the God of peace Himself <u>sanctify you</u> **completely**; and may your **<u>whole</u>** <u>spirit</u>, <u>soul</u>, and <u>body</u> be preserved <u>blameless</u> at the coming of our Lord Jesus Christ.* (1 Thessalonians 5:23 emphases added)

SPIRITUAL HEARING EXERCISE:

If you are someone that has not prayed in the spirit and is desiring to do so, first, you need to understand, that there is a type of spiritual prayer that is personal, private, and available to everyone. *He who speaks in a tongue does not speak to men but to God…in the spirit he speaks <u>mysteries</u>…He who speaks in a tongue <u>edifies himself</u>.* (1 Corinthians 14:2-4 emphases added) *Likewise the Spirit also helps in our weaknesses. For we do not know what we should pray for as we ought, but the Spirit Himself makes intercession for us with groanings which cannot be uttered.* (Romans 8:26 emphases added)

ALL of us need edification, and God does show favoritism to one person being edified more than another, therefore this self-edification capability is given to us all through the Spirit. (Romans 2:11)

Inappropriate expectations established within our beliefs can mentally erect barriers to releasing the flow of this spiritual prayer language. Oftentimes, people desiring to pray in the spirit, are told by their spouse that they speak in tongues while sleeping. This is because it is easy for their spirit to pray while their mind is at rest.

Concentrate your attention on two things at the same time, this may seem impossible, but it's an ability you already possess. It's like listening to someone explaining an idea, and at the same time thinking of other ideas related to what is being said. Initially, it may seem like your attention is jumping back and forth between thoughts, but with time it will become easier. This is a capability your spirit possesses.

- Close your eyes, and while thinking of the prayer and scripture of the day, try to imagine hearing the "sound" of a spiritual prayer. This is like reciting in your mind a verse that you've memorized while listening to music in the background.
- Within your imagination, attempt to clearly identify the phonetic sounds of the spiritual prayer you're imagining; example:

BooWeDoe

- While thinking of the prayer or scripture verse, try to follow the phonetic sounds you are hearing. Has anyone ever asked you, are you listening to me, and you were able to recite everything they said even though you were thinking of something else?

- Eventually, you'll notice your ability to think on the prayer or scripture of the day, while attentively following the phonetic sounds you are hearing in that spiritual prayer.

- The next step is to continue thinking on the prayer or scripture of the day, while softly attempting to verbalize the phonetic sounding spiritual prayer. Treat this as if it was leading you in prayer. Eventually, you'll become fluent in reciting the phonetic sounds you're hearing.

If you enjoyed reading this book, please leave a review online at our website or the online store where you purchased the book. I do my best to read all reviews and reply to questions.

About the Author

Jose J Sanchez is a minister of the gospel known for his simplified method of explaining mysteries of the kingdom. The LORD also bearing witness *both with signs and wonders, with various miracles, and gifts of the Holy Spirit* done by his hands followings his teachings. (Hebrew 2:4, Acts 14:2)

Jose is the founder of Christ Revealed Academy and serves as an Associate Pastor at Christ Revealed Embassy, a School of Ministry church, in Maryland, USA, under the leadership of Senior Pastors, Paul and Mona Sherrill.

For additional information, publications, video and audio sermons, visit: www.JoseSanchez.org

CPSIA information can be obtained
at www.ICGtesting.com
Printed in the USA
LVHW010856130421
684340LV00019B/955